Baby Animals with Their Families

SUZI ESZTERHAS

Owlkids Books

Animal families come in all shapes and sizes. But no matter what kind of family they have, babies need care and support from others as they learn and grow. Let's meet some baby animals and their families!

Chimpanzees live in big communities. They help take care of one another and do everything together, from playing and eating, to sleeping.

Lion families are called prides. Father lions are always on the lookout for danger. It's a serious job, but this cub makes sure Dad takes a break for some fun. Come on, let's play!

Albatross families include one mom, one dad, and one chick. The chicks in this colony all look the same, but parents know which chick belongs to them. If they get separated, they can find their baby with a special call.

Topi live and travel in herds. Herds work together to keep everyone, especially the calves, safe from predators.

Baby polar bears are born in litters of two to four cubs. These triplets stay warm and cozy on Mom's soft fur. Thanks, Mom!

Humpback whales live alone but meet up with other whales when they are ready to have babies. This newborn calf stays close to Mom. Sometimes older family members swim nearby to keep them safe, too.

Sloths live in small families—just one mother and one baby. Until this young sloth is strong enough to hang from branches on her own, she rides on Mom's chest.

Elephant babies live with their brothers, sisters, cousins, moms, aunts, and grandmothers. The family has many ways of communicating but their favorite way to say hello is with a trunk hug. Hi, Auntie!

These cheetah siblings love to play with one another. But their mother wants them to pay attention and stay close by while she looks for food.

Baby bat-eared foxes stay safe in their family's hidden den while their parents hunt for food. When Mom and Dad return, it's family snuggle time. Sweet dreams, babies!

Suzi Eszterhas

I spent two months photographing these tigers in India. I got to watch the adorable cubs grow!

Hi, I'm Suzi!

I travel all over the world taking pictures of animals. I also help animal conservationists by telling their stories and raising money for their causes. When I'm not snapping photos, I like talking to people about how they can help wild animals. I think it's important for kids to connect with animals and nature. You can do this by looking at photos, reading books, or just going outside with your family to play and explore your world like these baby animals!

When this baby hippo got tired of swimming, it stopped for a rest on Mom. Time for a snooze!

Normally it's dangerous to get this close to brown bears. But we were able to photograph these bear families at a conservation center because they were used to humans.

This is me with my dog, Puppers. I rescued him when he was a homeless puppy, and he quickly became a member of my family.

Ring-tailed lemurs live in groups called troops. The babies ride on their mothers' backs until they are old enough to jump around on their own.

I was so happy when I got to photograph this tiny baby rhino. She looked just like a miniature version of her mother.

A group of giraffes is called a tower. That makes perfect sense because this baby giraffe was already six feet tall at birth!

When penguins are ready to have babies, they live together in giant colonies. These brown chicks were so cute.

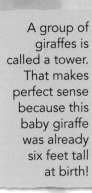

This swan family lives in my neighborhood. I first saw the parents when they were sitting on a nest of eggs. I was so excited to see six fluffy babies had finally hatched!

Text and photographs © 2019 Suzi Eszterhas
First printing in paperback, 2022

Consultant: Chris Earley, Interpretive Biologist, University of Guelph Arboretum

Owlkids Books acknowledges the financial support of the Canada Council for the Arts, the Ontario Arts Council, the Government of Canada through the Canada Book Fund (CBF), and the Government of Ontario through the Ontario Creates Book Initiative for our publishing activities.

Published in Canada by
Owlkids Books Inc.
1 Eglinton Avenue East
Toronto, ON M4P 3A1

Published in the United States by
Owlkids Books Inc.
1700 Fourth Street
Berkeley, CA 94710

Library and Archives Canada Cataloguing in Publication

Title: Baby animals with their families / Suzi Eszterhas.
Names: Eszterhas, Suzi, author, photographer.
Description: Previously published: 2019.
Identifiers: Canadiana 20210377437 | ISBN 9781771475778 (softcover)
Subjects: LCSH: Familial behavior in animals—Pictorial works—Juvenile literature. | LCSH: Animals—Infancy—Pictorial works—Juvenile literature.
Classification: LCC QL761.5 .E89 2022 | DDC j591.56/3—dc23

Library of Congress Control Number: 2018944998

Edited by Jackie Farquhar
Designed by Danielle Arbour

ONTARIO ARTS COUNCIL
CONSEIL DES ARTS DE L'ONTARIO
an Ontario government agency
un organisme du gouvernement de l'Ontario

Canada Council
for the Arts

Conseil des Arts
du Canada

Canadä

Manufactured in Guangdong Province, Dongguan City, China, in February 2022, by Toppan Leefung Packaging & Printing (Dongguan) Co., Ltd.
Job #BAYDC59/R1

B   C   D   E   F   G

FSC
MIX
Paper from
responsible sources
FSC® C104723

 Publisher of Chirp, Chickadee and OWL
www.owlkidsbooks.com

Owlkids Books is a division of bayard canada